Snakes and Crocs and other reptiles

LEVEL 2 READER

READING LEVEL
2
GRADES 1 TO 3

Written by Kathryn Knight
Illustrated by Edizioni Larus S.p.A.

The BENDON name and logo are trademarks of Bendon
Ashland, OH 44805 • 1-888-5-BENDON
bendonpub.com

Rattlesnake

What's that rattling sound coming from behind that desert rock? It's a rattlesnake! Don't be fooled by its thick body. This reptile is fast! It strikes with two sharp fangs.

This snake's rattle is made of dry scales left over each time the snake *molts* (sheds its skin).

Milk Snake

Look at these two snakes. They look alike. But only one of them is *venomous* (poisonous).

The milk snake has bands of color—black, yellow, black, then red. It is not venomous. It squeezes and eats mice, reptiles, and birds.

Coral Snake

The coral snake also has bands of color—black, yellow, red, yellow, black, yellow. This snake has fangs—and it is venomous! It eats small mammals, birds, and insects.

Water Moccasin

This venomous snake is also called a cottonmouth. It is common in swamps, lakes, and rivers in the Southern United States. Its bite can be *fatal* (can kill a person). Never go near a water moccasin! It is an excellent swimmer and can grow to 5 or 6 feet long.

Yellow-bellied Sea Snake

Some snakes live in the water. The yellow-bellied sea snake lives in warm waters around the world. It has a flat "paddle" tail to help it swim. It stays near the surface to get air.

This snake is very poisonous. When a shark sees its yellow color, it stays away!

Boa Constrictor

The boa constrictor is a big snake. It can grow to 13 feet long. It spends most of its time coiled around a branch in a forest of Central or South America.

When a small animal walks by, the boa reaches out and grabs it with its mouth. Then it wraps it in a deadly hug. It will swallow the animal whole!

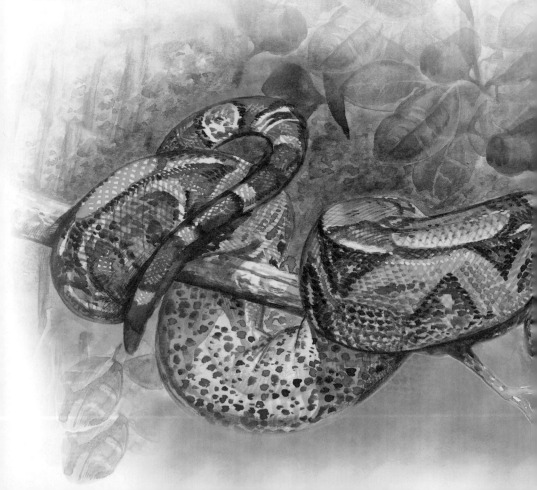

Python

The python is another large snake— 3 to 20 feet long. Most live in rainforests around the world. Like the boa, the python

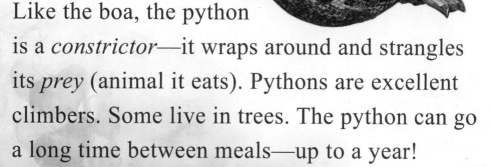

is a *constrictor*—it wraps around and strangles its *prey* (animal it eats). Pythons are excellent climbers. Some live in trees. The python can go a long time between meals—up to a year!

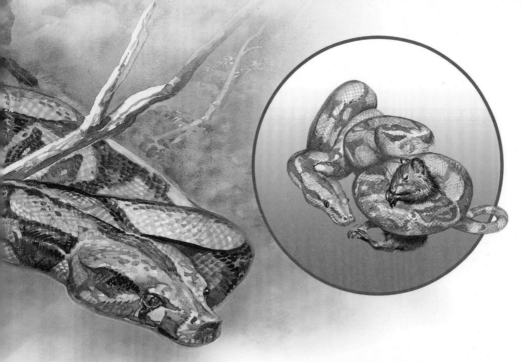

Anaconda

The anaconda is one of the largest snakes in the world. Some can be 36 feet long—or longer! Anacondas live near swamps and rivers in South America. They coil up on low branches or stay in the water, watching for prey. They are constrictors. They eat deer and other mammals, birds, fish, and turtles. Never let an anaconda give you a hug!

The king cobra is the longest poisonous snake. It can grow to 18 feet long. The king cobra can make the skin around its neck very wide. This scares away other animals.

When the king cobra strikes at prey, it hisses loudly. It has fangs that put poison into its prey. It likes to eat other snakes!

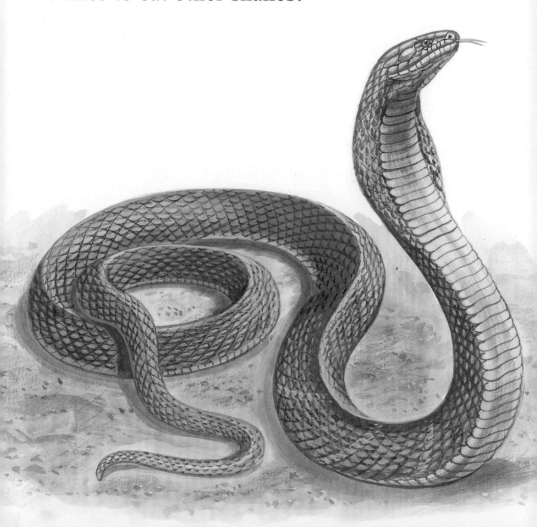

African Crocodile

Crocodiles are large reptiles. They can grow to 16 feet long and weigh as much as a small car! They have thick, scaly skin and powerful jaws.

The African (or Nile) crocodile lives in and near rivers and lakes. The crocodile waits for a zebra, bird, or other animal to come drink at the shore. Then it strikes with a *snap* of its sharp teeth!

Baby crocs hatch from eggs. The mother protects them until they can live on their own.

The crocodile's nose, eyes, and ears are on the top of its head. It can stay just under the top of the water—and no one will see it!

American Crocodile

The American crocodile lives in the swamps of the Americas. There are not many left in the wild in Florida. Crocodiles have a slender snout. When a croc's mouth is closed, some of its top teeth and also its bottom teeth come out over the lips—like a creepy smile!

American Alligator

The American alligator is the biggest reptile in North America. It lives along the southern coasts and in some rivers. The alligator has a wide snout. When its mouth is closed, only the top teeth come out over the bottom lip. Alligators eat fish, small mammals, and birds.

Gavial

The gavial (**gay**-vee-uhl) lives in Asia.
It can grow to 20 feet long. Look how long and
thin its snout is! This helps it catch slippery fish.

Marine Crocodile

Australia is home to the biggest croc in the world. It can be 24 to 30 feet long! It lives in rivers and swamps. It also swims from island to island in the saltwater—so it is called a "saltie." It eats fish, crabs, and mammals—even big mammals. It can leap from the water to grab its prey!

Galapagos Tortoise

Have you ever seen a 200-pound turtle that's bigger than you? You can if you go to the Galapagos Islands near South America. A Galapagos tortoise (**tor**-tuss) moves slowly and eats slowly. It can live for 150 years!

Mata Mata Turtle

What is this odd reptile? It looks like it is made of wood—or maybe it's a rock with seaweed on it. It's a mata mata turtle! It stays underwater all day waiting for food. It gets air by sticking its thin snout out of the water.

When a small fish or insect comes near, the mata mata opens its mouth and sucks it in. Slurp!

Loggerhead Sea Turtle

Loggerheads are large sea turtles. They can weigh 300 pounds. They have big heads and powerful jaws that crush crabs, clams, and other shellfish.

A mother loggerhead lays about 500 eggs in the sand on the beach. When all those baby loggerheads hatch, it's quite a sight! All over the beach, tiny turtles dig out of the sand and scurry to the water.

Snapping Turtle

Some turtles make great pets. But not this one! The snapping turtle has sharp claws and a hard bite. It can weigh up to 80 pounds.

A snapping turtle will hide in a pond or lake, waiting for a fishy meal. It quickly grabs it—snapping its jaw closed. It will also hunt birds and small mammals.

Chameleon

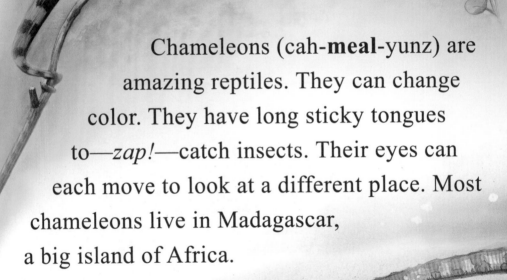

Chameleons (cah-**meal**-yunz) are amazing reptiles. They can change color. They have long sticky tongues to—*zap!*—catch insects. Their eyes can each move to look at a different place. Most chameleons live in Madagascar, a big island of Africa.

Basilisk

The basilisk (**bass**-uh-lisk) is a reptile that lives in South America near rivers and streams. It has large hind feet with flaps of skin between each toe. When this lizard wants to get away, it just skitters right across the top of the water on its webbed feet!

Gila Monster

The Gila (**hee**-luh) monster is a big
lizard that lives in the American desert.
It is a beautiful lizard—but, stay away!
Its bite is poisonous!

Horned Toad

The horned toad is not a toad at all. It's
a lizard. This little dragon lives in the desert.
It loves to eat ants. If you pick it up, it will
squirt blood at
you from its eyes!

Galapagos Iguanas

The iguanas (ig-**wahn**-uhz) of the Galapagos Islands are big lizards. Some live in the water. They eat algae (**al**-gee) that grow on rocks.

Marine iguana

Others live on land. The land iguana warms itself in the sun and then digs a den in the earth when it needs to cool off. It eats plants.

Land iguana

Komodo Dragon

Here is a real dragon! It is the largest lizard in the world, growing 10 feet long. The Komodo dragon lives on an island of Indonesia. Its bite delivers deadly venom! It eats big animals— so don't be draggin' your feet near this dragon!